Hedgerah Lv. Lwood

A MEDLEY OF YOUTHFUL VERSES

By

KETURAH W. WOOD

THE GOLDEN QUILL PRESS
Publishers
Francestown   New Hampshire

Library of Congress Catalog Card Number 93-90018

ISBN 0-8233-0484-1

Printed in the United States of America

*Dedicated
to my daughter Elsa
in appreciation of her helpful support.*

ACKNOWLEDGEMENTS

Poems by the Author have appeared in *The Villager*, *Alura*, *Candelabrum*, *The Eclectic Muse*, *Yearbook of Modern Poetry 1976*, and the first poem of this volume, "Caprice," was published previously in *Lyrical Voices*. Two of her haiku have been published by World of Poetry and two small volumes of verse by Valkyrie Press.

CONTENTS

A MEDLEY OF YOUTHFUL VERSES

CAPRICE

Fairy lilies, waving bells,
Carven bells of white,
Sound your chimes across the dells
In the evening light.

Softly sound your elfin tones
Through the piney wild
Till they're caught among the cones
By a fairy child.

INVITATION

Dark was my mood,
Bird on the wing,
When you flew by
One morning in spring.

So brilliant your color,
So gay your flight,
You gave to me
A moment of light.

O nest nearby,
Bird on the wing,
And flash by my window
Each morning in spring.

THE MOTHER BIRD

I watch you pass
Above the grass,
Bird so spry,
But soon alight
To banish fright
Where nestlings lie.

I mark you fill
Each tiny bill
With worms you bring.
Then I delight,
O bird of flight,
To hear you sing!

FOR SPRING AND SUMMER

Lightly on the linden tree
You are frisking merrily.
Welcome, leaflets, as you bring
All the joy of wakening spring.

You who wing in evening hours
Above the dreaming summer flowers
Are welcome, fireflies, as you throw
Everywhere your fitful glow.

THE SONG

On a magic night in June
Our mother sang this song:
"Tie a ribbon to the moon,
A silver ribbon long.

Pull the moon across the sky.
Where's a gayer sight
Than the young moon sailing by
To a child's delight?

Gather the fallen stars and keep
Them with the moonlight's beams,
And when a child has gone to sleep
They'll steal into his dreams."

QUESTIONS

Winsome fairies flitting by
On tiny, twinkling toes,
Do you build your summer bowers
With petals from a rose?

Do you gather crimson leaves
When they start to fall,
And stitch them into silken gowns
For your winter ball?

POEM BY A CHILD

Roses bloom in June.
First peeps out of the dark ground
On this beautiful earth so wide and round
Something green, then further it grows
Till on its stem blooms a beautiful rose.

BLOSSOMS

Skimming lightly over grass,
Catching sunbeams as they pass,
Lovely as a bridal veil
Are blossoms blown along the trail.

SAND CASTLES

At noon we built upon the beach
Castles out of ocean's reach
And found, before another day,
The sea had washed each one away.

We thought our castles could withstand
All assaults against the land,
But alas! the tide was strong,
And they were brusquely swept along.

LONG JOURNEYS

You'll fly above the ocean
To visit foreign land
Where gray cliffs are rising
Above a foreign strand,

While I, upon the dunes,
Shall try to paint the sea.
Do you know adventure
Awaits both you and me?

GYPSY LULLABIES

1.

Tossing tree on verdant lea,
Bird call ringing clear,
Running rill, churning mill
Waft my baby cheer,
Banish every fear.

2.

Breeze so bland on sea and land,
Wavelet of the deep,
Soft refrain of cooling rain
Waft my baby sleep,
Gentle vigil keep.

WAITING

Some children fall asleep at night
Sailing on the sea,
But an engine, colored blue,
Always stops for me.

It has to call for several friends
And sometimes can be late,
So I picture all its route
While I lie and wait.

My engine runs through tunnels first,
Past gates and signal towers;
Past tall buildings dimmed by smoke,
Past meadows gay with flowers.

When at last it turns around
To hurry down my way,
"Toot-toot" is the cheery sound
That I hear it say.

My playmates all are laughing now,
Laughing more and more
As my engine softly chugs
Around my bedroom door.

Puffing hard across the room,
It whistles and slows down.
I hear the children calling me,
"Get on for Slumber Town!"

CONSOLATIONS

Mary Sue is sick in bed,
But there's a pleasant time ahead.
Soon her mother will appear,
Her gentle face aglow with cheer.
From her basket she will draw
A pretty puppet made of straw—
A bewitching little thing
Bouncing up and down on string.
Then when Daddy comes from town,
He will bring a funny clown
With cheeks so white and nose so red,
Mary Sue will laugh instead
Of feeling sorry she must stay
Bed-fast for another day.

IN THE RAIN

Emma Lou, put on your boots
And button up your coat.
We'll go down beside the pond
To see the ducks afloat.

There are others on the bank
Which move in single file,
Waddling in their funny way
And quacking all the while.

These water fowl are pretty birds
With wing patches of blue.
It will be fun to visit them;
Please come, Emma Lou.

And bring your red umbrella too!

MY NEIGHBOR

You scamper off as fast as you can
Whenever I come near.
Why are you afraid of me?
What is there to fear?

Can't you see that I'm someone
Who never does you harm?
It doesn't make good sense at all
That you show alarm.

Don't you know I'm only a girl
Who talks to you each day?
So why in the world, you funny squirrel,
Why do you run away?

REWARD

My little pussy cat
Was in a dreadful plight
When someone threw her out
From a car one night.

I took her home with me
And gently stroked her fur
Before I gave her milk
That seemed to comfort her.

My little pussy cat
Has brought me much delight
Since I found her crying
On the road that night—
My little pussy cat,
So beautiful and white.

CHAGRIN

Fleet had six burrs on his ear.
He let me gather four.
Then off he ran to visit Pete,
The frisky dog next door.

Pete welcomed him with joyful barks.
That he wanted him to play,
But those burrs so bothered Fleet
That he could not stay.

He wandered home—a downcast dog—
And showed in every way
That he was sorry he had run
Away from home today,
His wistful eyes entreating me
To take those burrs away.

THE PROPRIETOR

Jeanna, what do you suppose
That I saw today?
An animal walked past our house
As if he owned the way!

He was a handsome passer-by
In a coat of black and gray.
A friendly dog or pussy cat,
Did I hear you say?

No, he wasn't a friendly dog
Or a pussy cat
But an animal you've seldom seen—
I am sure of that.

He was ousted from his nest
Under a neighbor's roof.
Now can you guess just what he was?
Do you need more proof?

Grandfather's clock is striking twelve.
You'll be leaving soon,
So I shall tell you right away:
He was a bold racoon.

Yes, he was a bold racoon
In a coat of black and gray.
As confident of himself he was
As if he owned the way!

HAVOC

The wind was a lion attacking its prey
As it swept the garbage cans away.
Roll and rumble, roll and rumble,
All along and beyond the road;
Roll and rumble, roll and rumble,
Wildly flew each garbage load!
It wasn't an evil wind at all
That fiercely raged on every street,
For laughing children clapped their hands
And barking dogs had much to eat.
Roll and rumble, roll and rumble,
Never was known such a windy day!
Roll and rumble, roll and rumble,
The garbage all has gone astray.

THE TOY SHOP

Today I found inside a store—
The one beside the mall—
A rabbit in blue over-alls
Standing very tall;
A dolly rocking on a chair,
All her sewing done,
And pussy chasing spools of thread—
What a world of fun!
There were engines drawn in line
Ready for a fire,
And last of all an angel child
Playing on a lyre.

PLAYTIME

1.

Children fly their crimson kites—
Paper birds—on high,
That dance about like jumping jacks
Underneath the sky.

2.

Flitting clouds that half conceal
Distant hills of blue,
Were the children taught to play
Hide-and-seek by you?

IN THE SHOE REPAIR STORE

Said the slippers red to the slippers brown
"Today we're going to the center of town,
And upon our lady's feet
We'll go tripping along the street.
Some time later we will stop
And go into a candy shop.
Then tonight we slippers red
Will sleep beneath our lady's bed.

Slippers Brown, what will you do
When your lady comes for you?"
"We'll run and run across the floor:
Our little lady's only four.
When she mounts her hobby horse
We will move along its course
And upon her scooter ride
Across the room from side to side.

When will your lady come for you?
Won't you tell us, Slippers Blue?"
"She'll be coming very soon
Because we're going this afternoon
To see the circus now in town.
There will be a red-nosed clown,
Some elephants and monkeys too,
And perhaps a kangaroo.
We'll have more fun than both of you,"
Said the haughty slippers blue.

"Don't be so sure," said the slippers gold.
"We're sure the others haven't told
All the wonderful things they'll do.
Be more modest, Slippers Blue."

KEEPSAKES

It's been raining very hard.
We have spent the day
Poking round the storage room
Where things are put away.

There were pictures we had drawn
When only six or seven—
Pictures of wild thunderstorms
And rainbows up in heaven.

We found our mother's china doll,
Our great-grandmother's shawl,
A long-forgotten Ping Pong set,
A long-lost basketball.

What fun we had re-reading tales
Of gypsies and of kings.
Oh, yes, our storage room is full
Of delightful things!

NOCTURNE

Every night and all night long,
Loudly the cricket is chirping his song.
Has he a message he wishes to tell,
Or does he rejoice that all is well?
Whatever the reason his chirping will keep
All of the family unable to sleep,
But no one is sorry to stay awake:
He brings good fortune in his wake!

THE HOUSE

I am sorry for that house.
It looks extremely sad.
Something must have brought it grief,
Something really bad.

No fire has gutted its facade
Or despoiled its roof.
Robbers may have been inside,
But there is no proof.

Now it's coming back to me:
I heard a neighbor say
The owners sold that mournful house
And have moved away.

MYSTERY

When Ruth was passing a vacant house—
A large house built of stone—
She heard such growls as made her wish
She wasn't all alone.

She felt certain that the sounds
Were from the second floor.
Could it be she heard a lion
Or a tiger roar?

"Who are you?" she bravely called.
"What are you doing there?"
The answer came in taunting tones:
"Ha, ha, I am a bear!"

How strange, Ruth thought, the voice should sound
Like that of Billy Ware.
Could he be playing just a prank?
She wondered if he'd dare,
And proudly tossed her head on high
As if she didn't care.

MIGRANTS AND HOMEMAKERS

Welcome robins on the wing
Are bright harbingers of spring.
Flocks of wild geese winging high
Foretell autumn from the sky.

Different are the chickadees
Which dwell among our woodland trees;
They daily share with us their cheer,
Content to stay at home all year.

AMONG THE LEAVES

We splashed among the leaves today—
Crinkly leaves of brown—
That from lofty chestnut trees
Lightly tumbled down.

Overhead the wild geese flew
With many a raucous call,
As we splashed among brown leaves
And caught the tang of fall.

THE REPLY

Where does she find her verses?
Only this I know:
Some appear on sunbeams;
Others, drops of snow.

Some arrive on moon rays—
Waving forms of light.
They beckon her with magic
And haunt her through the night.

All that she has written
Softly bears the glow
Of regions filled with sunbeams,
Moon rays, and the snow.

INQUIRIES

1.

Burnished leaves that downward fly,
Thickly on the hard earth lie,
Do you remember the mantle so green
You gave to the trees all gray and lean?

2.

Under ground now white with snow,
Bulbs in hiding, do you know
You'll be daffodils some day,
Gladdening all who pass your way?

WIND OF WINTER

Up and down and up you go,
Ragged leaves across the snow.
Hear the wind of winter shout
As it tosses you about.

Wildly you spin above the hedge,
Rising up to my window ledge.
Hear the wind of winter sigh
As it carries you on high.

Over the road you madly prance,
Whirling around in a gypsy dance.
Hear the wind of winter blow
As it whisks you to and fro.

THE SOLUTION

Jean has trouble going to sleep.
Joan has trouble too
Because their feet stay very cold
No matter what they do.

Jean knows how to tie a knot;
Joan knows how to thread,
So they help each other make
Socks to wear in bed.

There'll be many a freezing night
But Joan and Jean will sleep all right.

AN OLD-FASHIONED RIDE

Snow had covered all the ground
When on a winter day,
Our uncle took us for a ride
In the scarlet sleigh.

Clear the sound of jingling bells
As Dusky sped away,
With snowflakes frisking everywhere
Around the scarlet sleigh.

Merrily skating, the country folk,
Scarved in red and gray,
Waved to us as we rode by
In the scarlet sleigh.

The air was growing colder still,
But we kept on our way
While faster, thicker flew the flakes
Around the scarlet sleigh.

Snow had covered all the ground
When on a winter day,
Our uncle took us for a ride
In the scarlet sleigh.

DECEMBER TWENTY FOURTH

Some time before her saint is due
To clamber down the chimney flue,
Betsy Ann is going to bake
A double decker cherry cake.
On the icing she will write
Carefully in red and white,
"A present for you—just because
It's Christmas Eve, dear Santa Claus!"

THE VISIT

On Christmas tree the candle glow
Falls on balls and tinsel throw.
Peeking from each stocking top
Are candy cane and lollipop.
By the chimney there's a sled
And a wagon painted red.
Here's a doll with henna hair
(Dresses, too, for her to wear)
Come see the lamb all soft and white.
Why, Santa Claus was here last night!

A CHRISTMAS DREAM

Gentle angel all in white
On my Christmas tree,
I dreamt you fluttered down last night
And talked a while with me.

You told me you had travelled far
From land across the sea
To hang with balls beneath the star
On my Christmas tree.

An artist's touch filled you with light,
You said wonderingly,
Gentle angel all in white
On my Christmas tree.

THE CARDINAL

Just beyond my window sill
The evening snow is falling still.
In the morning there will be
Fallen snow on every tree,
On the hedges, on the ground,
Whitening all the world around—
All except a bird in red
Perking up his pretty head
As if he proudly wants to show
His brilliant coat against the snow.

COLD MORNING

Crystal leaves all glistening
On my window pane,
Was Jack Frost the artist
Who left you in his train?

Crystal leaves all glistening
In the morning light,
Will you melt away
Before the fall of night?

Crystal leaves all glistening,
If you must depart,
I shall keep your image
Always in my heart.

THE WELCOME

Gentle snowflakes falling
Since your distant birth,
Do you hear her calling,
Hear the kindly Earth?

She has seen you turning
Downward in your flight,
Knows that you are yearning
For haven through the night.

Forth her love is welling.
Surely you must know
She will give you dwelling,
Gentle flakes of snow.

THEIR MAJESTIES

Only patches now are left
Of the drifted snow,
But the sky is turning gray,
And we can but know
That another storm will be
Hastening, hurtling down
To place upon each stately tree
An imperial crown.

HOME

I'm the only leaf on the maple tree,
And I intend to stay
Although the wind is doing its best
To carry me away.

That ruthless wind has wildly swept
All of my mates from me,
But I shall stay because my heart
Lies in the maple tree.

THE VISITOR

A gentle bluebird flew to me
On a winter day,
A bird so dear I could not help
Inviting her to stay.

I made my living room her home,
I gave her food and drink,
And we forged between us two
A most delightful link.

But when spring had come, I felt
She did not wish to stay,
And so I opened wide the door
And bade her fly away.

I am hoping that next year
When birds will southward flee,
My gentle bluebird will decide
To come home to me.

MUSICAL MOMENT

There is a golden strain
Upon the air afloat:
The morning song arising
From an oriole's golden throat.

TRANSFORMATION

Silently great golden leaves
Depart upon the air,
Leaving empty every bough
Until the tree is bare.

Although each bough has been bereft
Of golden leaves today,
The tree will still be beautiful
In all its naked gray.

NOBILITY

Is not in every tree—
Tall and great and free—
A spirit living
That bids the branches high
Strive to part the sky,
Visions giving?

C O L O P H O N

This book is one of an edition of
six hundred fifty copies
printed and bound at The Golden Quill Press,
in the year nineteen-hundred ninety-three.
The text is set in a digital facsimile
of a typeface designed in 1540 by
Geofroy Tory's pupil, Claude Garamond,
on command of Francois I of France.
The text paper, Smyth-sewn in sixteen page signatures,
is Mohawk Mills' sixty-pound basis acid-free
Mohawk Cream White Vellum, manufactured at
Cohoes, New York.

This infinity symbol ∞
represents Golden Quill's commitment to quality paper stock,
which will last several centuries,
and our cooperation with
The National Information Standards Organization, Washington, DC.